TABLE TIME

TABLE TIME

The exciting new way to learn multiplication tables

Susan McDougall

Illustrations by Helen Thomas

HARRAP

London

First published in Great Britain 1990
by HARRAP BOOKS Ltd
Chelsea House, 26 Market Square,
Bromley, Kent BR1 1NA

Text © Susan McDougall 1990
Illustrations © Harrap Books Ltd 1990

ISBN 0 245–60034–5

Printed in Spain by Jerez Industrial, S.A.

Contents

Let's meet
the numbers

Have you noticed that if you draw an eight it looks just like a fat lady?
All the other numbers you meet when you are learning your tables have characters too.

0 is a ghost: he is going oooooo and lots more oooooos are coming out of his mouth.

1 is an old-fashioned mirror; the sort that has legs and stands up by itself.

2 is a beautiful swan with a long graceful neck.

3 is the thin lady; she looks like that because she is always on a diet.

4 is a sailing boat.

5 is a man with a fat tummy; his tummy is fat because he eats so many baked beans.

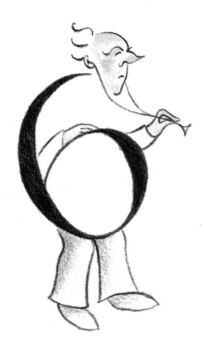

6 is the doctor.

7 is a little girl with a pony tail; she's always in trouble.

8 is our fat lady again.

9 is a man with a big nose; not only is it big, it's also rather red.

10 is a magic hen with its magic egg.

11 is the terrible twins.

12 looks like a man with a wand. 12 is the magician.

The adventures
of the ghost

Some ghosts are happy but the ghost in our story was always miserable because all he could say was oooooo. Because he was such a miserable ghost, he simply couldn't bear to see anybody who was happier than him. As everybody was happier than him, he couldn't bear to see anybody at all. Though he could only say oooooo, he did have one other power. He could make things disappear so there was nothing left of them at all.

He made the mirror disappear.
0 × 1 = 0

He made the swan disappear.
0 × 2 = 0

He made the thin lady disappear.
0 × 3 = 0

He made the sailing boat disappear.
0 × 4 = 0

He made the man with the fat tummy disappear.
0 × 5 = 0

He made the doctor disappear.
0 × 6 = 0

He made the little girl with the pony tail disappear.
$$0 \times 7 = 0$$

He made the fat lady disappear.
$$0 \times 8 = 0$$

He made the man with the big nose disappear.
$$0 \times 9 = 0$$

He made the magic hen and her egg disappear
and the terrible twins and the magician.
$$0 \times 10 = 0$$
$$0 \times 11 = 0$$
$$0 \times 12 = 0$$

He did not stop there.
He made every number he met disappear.

He made a 33 disappear.
$$0 \times 33 = 0$$

He made a 98 disappear.
$$0 \times 98 = 0$$

He made 5,658 disappear.
$$0 \times 5{,}658 = 0$$

He even made a billion trillion zillion quintillion
disappear.
$$0 \times \textbf{a billion trillion zillion quintillion} = 0$$

If you can think of a bigger number, he could
make that disappear too. But it would still not
make him happy.

The adventures of the mirror

The mirror was a truthful mirror. It always showed what was there; nothing more, nothing less.

If the ghost looked in the mirror before he made it disappear, he just saw himself.

$$1 \times 0 = 0$$

Another mirror was placed in front of our mirror. In the glass you could see the other mirror.

$$1 \times 1 = 1$$

When the swan looked in the mirror it too saw itself.

$$1 \times 2 = 2$$

The little girl with the pony tail peeped in and saw her own face grinning back.

$$1 \times 7 = 7$$

The magician found that it was not a magic mirror. All he saw was himself.

$$1 \times 12 = 12$$

A 53 looked in the mirror; it saw itself.

$$1 \times 53 = 53$$

A 472 looked in the mirror; it saw 472.

$$1 \times 472 = 472$$

A 3,689 looked in the mirror; it saw 3,689.

$$1 \times 3,689 = 3,689$$

A million million looked in the mirror.
It saw a million million.

$$1 \times \text{a million million} = \text{a million million}$$

The adventures
of the swan

The swan met a ghost
and it made him disappear.

$$2 \times 0 = 0$$

The swan looked in the mirror
and saw himself.

$$2 \times 1 = 2$$

2 x 2

The swan was paddling along the river admiring his own reflection when he noticed another swan paddling along behind. The first swan turned to the right; so did the second swan. The first swan turned to the left; so did the second swan. The first swan turned upside down in the water. So did the second swan. The first swan was annoyed.

"What are you copying me for?" he asked.

The second swan smiled in a swan-like way.

"What are you copying me **for**?"

What are you copying me FOR ?

for sounds like **4**
2 × 2 = 4

2 x 3

The swan was feeling very hungry. He saw the thin lady sitting on a bench near the river.

"Aha," he thought, "a person. I hope she will throw me some crusts."

He paddled up and down in front of her and stared at her with his beady eyes. Suddenly she threw something into the water. The swan saw the splash and paddled quickly towards it. When he saw that it was nothing but a stick he reared up and splashed the thin lady with his wings.

"Stupid thin lady," he honked, "I wanted bread not **sticks**."

Oh no ~ I'm soaked!

I wanted bread not STICKS!

sticks sounds like **6**
2 × 3 = 6

2 x 4

The swan was feeling tired, when he saw the sailing boat sailing across the lake.

"If I'm clever," he thought, "I could hang on to the boat with my beak and it would pull me along."

Very quietly the swan paddled closer and closer to the sailing boat and finally caught hold of a rope which was hanging over the boat's side. But the sailing boat had seen him coming. The moment he had caught hold, the boat pushed out its sails and went speeding across the lake as fast as it could, dragging the poor frightened swan behind. When the boat finally stopped, the swan was exhausted and a long way from land.

"Next time," laughed the boat, "ask where I'm going before you take a ride."

"There won't be a next time," said the swan, "you're the kind of boat I **hate**."

You're the kind of boat I HATE!

hate sounds like **8**

$2 \times 4 = 8$

2 x 5

The swan was admiring himself in the water when he noticed the man with the fat tummy walking along. The swan felt extremely proud of himself and proud of his figure.

"Look at me," he said to the man with the fat tummy. "Have you ever seen anything so beautiful? Aren't you sorry your tummy is so fat? Wouldn't you rather look like me?"

"Well," said the man with the fat tummy, "you seem a funny sort of shape to me."

"I'm not," said the swan indignantly.

"Your beak is too big," said the man with the fat tummy, "and your neck is too long."

"It is not," cried the swan, "it is not, it is not. All swans have long necks."

"Oh, a swan," said the man with the fat tummy, "then that explains it. I thought you were a funny looking **hen**."

I thought you were a HEN!

hen sounds like **10**
2 × 5 = 10

2 x 6

The swan was feeling poorly so he went to see the doctor. The doctor was busy.

"I'm not an animal doctor," he said crossly.

"And I'm not an animal," said the swan proudly.

"I'm not a bird doctor either," said the doctor, "so you can just fly away."

"I haven't any energy," moaned the swan. "I need a tonic, I can't fly."

The doctor was not impressed; he had seen moaning swans before. He gave a crafty smile.

"I have just the tonic for you," he said.

But instead of a bottle of medicine, he picked up a gun. The swan gave a loud squawk and flew straight out of the surgery window. The doctor laughed, and put the gun back behind the door.

"Best tonic I know," he said. "It always makes them **well**."

It always makes them WELL !

well sounds like **12**
2 × 6 = 12

2 x 7

The swan was lying asleep by the river bank when along came the little girl with the pony tail. She had a bow and arrow in her hand.

"That swan's tail feathers would be just right for my arrows," she thought.

She crept up behind the swan and with a sharp pull tugged out two large feathers. The swan woke up with a start. The little girl with the pony tail began to run away but the swan was too fast for her and he caught hold of her and gave her a nasty peck on the bottom.

"Don't! Stop it!" shrieked the little girl with the pony tail.

"I'll teach you to take my feathers" squawked the swan, giving her another peck.

"Please stop," the little girl with the pony tail pleaded. "It wasn't me. I didn't do anything."

"Who did then?" asked the swan.

The little girl thought for a minute.

"It was Jean," she said at length. "Jean did it."

The swan looked at his tail feathers which were still in her hand. He didn't believe a word of it. He gave her another peck.

"That one," he honked, "was **for Jean**."

If he pecks me again I'll cry!

That one was FOR JEAN!

for Jean sounds like **14**
2 × 7 = 14

2 x 8

It was Spring and the swan was paddling down the river looking for things to eat when he saw what looked like ten fat pink fishes. He was so busy looking at them that he didn't notice the fat lady, who was sitting on the bank with her toes dangling in the water. The ten fat pink fishes looked so inviting that the swan couldn't help himself and gave the biggest one a peck just to see what it tasted like.

The fat lady gave a very loud shriek: "Aggghhhh".

"I've never known fishes shriek before," said the swan. "What can it mean?"

"What does it mean?" shouted the fat lady. "It means you pecked my big toe, that's what it means."

She picked up a large stick and tried to hit the swan with it.

"Now I'm going to teach you something else. I'm going to teach you what **sticks mean**."

I've gone right off fish!

My poor toes!

I'll teach you what STICKS MEAN.

sticks mean sounds like **16**
2 × 8 = 16

2 x 9

It was a hot afternoon and the swan was lazily wandering along the bank of the river when he heard a funny noise coming from what looked like a bright red poppy.

"I've never known a poppy make such a funny noise before," thought the swan. "I'm going to tell it to stop."

He marched closer.

"Be quiet," he said sternly.

The noise continued. The swan leant forward and gave the poppy a sharp peck.

"Yarrooow," shouted the man with the big nose, waking up. "You pecked my nose."

The swan was embarrassed.

"I'm terribly sorry," he muttered, "I thought you were a snoring poppy. I do hope your nose doesn't hurt too much."

"Well it does hurt," said the man with the big nose. "Thanks to you, it's **aching**."

You pecked my nose!

How embarrassing.

It's ACHING.

aching sounds like **18**
$2 \times 9 = 18$

The magic hen lays an egg next to every number it sees.

$2 \times 10 = 20$

The terrible twins see everything double.

$2 \times 11 = 22$

2 x 12

The swan was wandering down by the marsh when he saw the tall pointed hat of the magician. The magician was carrying a huge cauldron and seemed to be muttering to himself. The swan paddled closer to hear what he was saying. The magician was reading an old spellbook.

"Frogspawn . . . three tablespoonfuls; got it. Newt spit . . . five drops; got it. Duckweed . . . a pinch; got it. All I need for my store of ingredients is a swan's tongue."

The swan felt himself turn cold and tried to paddle away. But the magician was too quick for him and grabbed him round the neck.

The swan struggled with all his might and broke away, upsetting the cauldron. Out dropped the frogspawn, the newt spit and the duckweed.

"You stupid swan," roared the magician, "I've a good mind to turn you into something. Look what you've done, look at my **empty store**!"

Look at my EMPTY STORE!

empty store sounds like **24**
2 × 12 = 24

The adventures of the thin lady

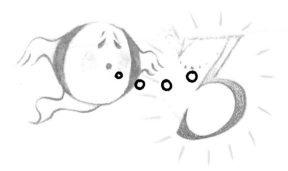

The thin lady met a ghost:
it made her disappear.

$$3 \times 0 = 0$$

The thin lady found a mirror, to see if she needed to lose more weight.
All she saw in it was herself, looking as slim as ever.

$$3 \times 1 = 3$$

3 x 2

The thin lady was sitting on a bench by the river reading a dieting magazine when along came the swan. It did not cross the thin lady's mind that the swan wanted food. She was pleased the swan seemed so friendly.

"What an intelligent looking bird," she thought. "I wonder whether he would like to play like a dog."

She threw a stick into the water, hoping that he would swim and fetch it. To her great surprise, the swan reared up and hissed at her.

"Stupid thin lady," he honked, "I wanted bread not **sticks**."

Oh no ~ I'm soaked !

1 wanted bread not STICKS !

sticks sounds like **6**
3 × 2 = 6

3 X 3

The thin lady arranged to meet another thin lady for tea in a café. The first thin lady was on time and sat down at a window table so that passers-by could admire her fine clothes and beautiful hat. Her friend was very late and the thin lady began to feel impatient.

At last she saw her friend, but to her horror the other thin lady was wearing an identical outfit to her own. She was wearing the same skirt, the same blouse, the same gloves, shoes and stockings and worst of all, the same wide-brimmed hat with an ostrich feather.

She was just wondering what to say, when her friend spoke first:

"My dear, you have excellent taste," she said.

The thin lady smiled icily and replied.

"You have excellent taste too, almost as good as **mine**."

Your taste is almost as good as MINE !

mine sounds like **9**
3 × 3 = 9

3 x 4

The thin lady went out to sea in a sailing boat. It was a lovely day and the sky was blue; there was a gentle breeze. The thin lady steered the boat out of the harbour, past the dangerous rocks, missed the shallow water, avoided a small rowing boat that got in the way, and all without getting her hair untidy or losing her hat.

"Have you ever sailed a boat before?" asked the boat.

"No," said the thin lady, "this is the first time."

"Then," said the boat, "you are doing very **well**."

You're sailing very WELL !

well sounds like **12**
3 × 4 = 12

3 x 5

The thin lady met the man with the fat tummy. As usual he was eating – this time it was baked beans.

The thin lady liked the man with the fat tummy, though she thought he ate too much.

"Hello, Old Bean," she said in a cheerful voice, "you look very fit."

"Yes," said the man with the fat tummy, "I've just come back from my holidays. I am a **fit bean**."

Yes, I am a FIT BEAN !

fit bean sounds like **15**
3 × 5 = 15

3 x 6

The thin lady went to the doctor as she was not feeling well.

"Doctor, I feel so faint," she said.

"I am not surprised," said the doctor. "I don't believe you eat enough. Tell me, what did you have for breakfast?"

"A boiled egg with salt, without the egg," said the thin lady.

"And what did you have for supper last night?" asked the doctor.

"A cucumber sandwich without the bread," replied the thin lady.

"And how about lunch yesterday?" asked the doctor.

"Oh, yesterday," answered the thin lady, "I had a treat. I had roast chicken and gravy . . ."

"I know," said the doctor, "without the chicken. But tell me, aren't you hungry?"

"Yes," said the thin lady, "my poor stomach is **aching**."

And my stomach is ACHING.

aching sounds like **18**
3 × 6 = 18

3 x 7

The thin lady took the little girl with the pony tail out to a cafe, but she forgot that children like a lot to eat. The thin lady ordered herself a cup of tea, without milk or sugar. Then she turned to the little girl with the pony tail.

"My dear," she said, "you may have a whole glass of lemonade to yourself."

When they had finished the thin lady took the little girl with the pony tail home in a taxi.

"Did you have a nice time?" she asked her.

"No," said the little girl with the pony tail, "I've got an **empty tum**."

There's nothing to eat...

Oh, my EMPTY TUM !

empty tum sounds like **21**
3 × 7 = 21

3 x 8

The thin lady went to the fat lady's house but the fat lady was not at home. In the garden there were a lot of birds flying around.

"Poor things," said the thin lady, "they do look hungry. I wonder if I can find them anything to eat."

She looked in the cupboard and found a store of cakes.

"I think these cakes may be stale," she said to herself, "and in any case the fat lady couldn't possibly want so many. I will feed them to the birds."

She had just finished scattering the last of the crumbs when the fat lady returned. To the thin lady's amazement, the fat lady was very upset and cried as though her heart would break.

"Oh dear," she sobbed, "what an **empty store**!"

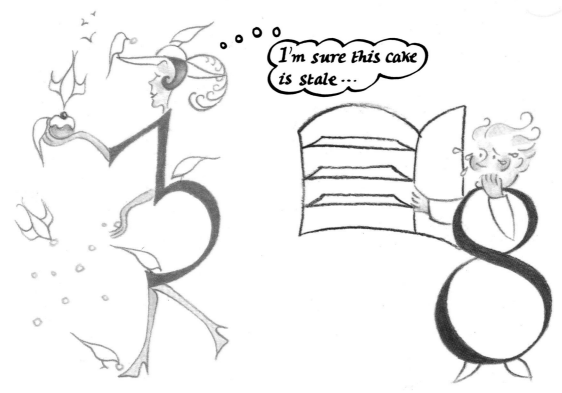

What an EMPTY STORE !

empty store sounds like **24**
3 × 8 = 24

3 x 9

The thin lady was fast asleep under a tree. She was awakened by a mighty sneeze. It was the man with the big nose.

"Oh my," she said, "I've just had a terrible dream."

"Tell me your dream," said the man with the big nose.

"Well," said the thin lady, "I dreamt that all the people in the world were told to go on a diet, and I was the only person in the world who kept to it. Then I dreamt I went to heaven and I was the only person there."

"You poor thing," said the man with the big nose, "you dreamt you were in an **empty heaven**."

I'm glad he woke me up.

Aaaatishoo!

You were in an EMPTY HEAVEN.

empty heaven sounds like **27**
3 × 9 = 27

The magic hen lays an egg next to every number it sees.

3 × 10 = 30

The terrible twins see everything double.

3 × 11 = 33

3 x 12

The thin lady was enjoying a drink of low calorie lemonade. Along came the magician. As usual he was in a bad mood.

"Give me your lemonade," he demanded.

"No," said the thin lady, "not when you are so extremely rude."

"Nobody says no to the magician," said the magician. "I will take it by magic."

And he did.

"But I am thirsty," cried the poor thin lady.

"I don't care," laughed the magician. "You should have given it to me straight away, and to punish you I am going to give you hiccups as well. Then you will have the **thirsty hics**!"

Oh no, not the THIRSTY HICS!

thirsty hics sounds like **36**
3 × 12 = 36

The adventures
of the sailing boat

The sailing boat met a ghost.
It made her disappear.

4 × 0 = 0

The sailing boat caught sight of herself in a mirror.
She saw herself.

4 × 1 = 4

4 x 2

The sailing boat was crossing the lake when she noticed the swan swimming towards her.

"I don't trust that swan," thought the sailing boat. "It's always out to get a free ride."

Then the sailing boat had an idea.

"I know, I'll teach it a lesson."

The sailing boat pretended not to see the swan, but when the swan grabbed a rope with its beak, the sailing boat spread out her sails and set off at high speed across the lake, pulling the swan behind her.

"It really is a remarkably stupid swan," the boat thought. "Why doesn't it just let go?"

But the swan did not let go. Finally the boat took pity on it and stopped.

"Next time," laughed the boat, "ask where I'm going before you take a ride."

It took a little time for the swan to answer because it was very puffed.

"Next time? There won't be a next time," said the swan. "You're the kind of boat I **hate**."

You're the kind of boat I HATE !

hate sounds like **8**
4 × 2 = 8

4 x 3

The sailing boat was waiting in the harbour for someone to take her out. Along came a thin lady.

"She doesn't look like much of a sailor," thought the sailing boat. "I do so hope that she doesn't scratch my nice new paint, or steer me onto the rocks, or leave me stranded on the mud."

But to her great surprise the thin lady sailed her safely out of the harbour and into the open sea. It was a lovely day. The sky was blue and there was a gentle breeze.

"Have you ever sailed a boat before?" the sailing boat asked her.

"No," said the thin lady.

"Then," said the sailing boat, "you are doing very **well**."

You're sailing very WELL !

well sounds like **12**
4 × 3 = 12

4 X 4

A sailing boat met another sailing boat. They decided to have a race. The first sailing boat started well and shot ahead as the wind filled her sails and blew her along. Suddenly the wind dropped. She found herself slowing down and then she stopped.

"Never mind," she thought to herself. "I'm still in front and the other boat won't be able to sail if there's no wind."

To her surprise the other boat brought out a funny pair of sticks and used them to paddle herself along. (Actually they were oars but the first sailing boat had led a sheltered life and did not know this.)

"What are you doing with those funny sticks?" asked the first sailing boat, who was very puzzled. "What does it all mean?"

The second sailing boat laughed out loud.

"Sticks," she roared, and nearly tipped over, she thought it was so funny. "I'm winning: that's what **sticks mean**."

That's what STICKS MEAN.

sticks mean sounds like **sixteen**
$$4 \times 4 = 16$$

4 X 5

The sailing boat was in the harbour when a man with a fat tummy came along. Beside the boat was a large notice which stated in red letters, 'This boat is only suitable for three persons'.

"I am only one person," he said to himself, "so I think I will get in."

The boat was worried.

"He looks far too heavy," she thought.

The man with the fat tummy jumped on board. The boat rocked violently and nearly went to the bottom.

The man with the fat tummy climbed out again.

"Suitable for three persons," he said, "what utter rubbish! What would have happened if someone else had been on board? Thank heavens it was **empty**."

Thank heavens it was EMPTY!

empty sounds like **20**
4 × 5 = 20

4 x 6

The sailing boat was in the harbour when along came the doctor. He climbed on board without asking anybody's permission.

"I don't like medical men," thought the sailing boat. "I think I will make this one a little seasick."

The sailing boat tossed about and soon the doctor felt queasy.

"I must find the First Aid Box and take a sea sickness tablet," said the doctor.

But he was in for a surprise. When he found the First Aid Box, there was nothing in it at all except for a single aspirin and a used piece of sticking plaster.

"How disgusting!" said the doctor. "There's supposed to be a proper First Aid Box in the ship's stores. This is an **empty store**."

I don't like doctors but this is embarrassing.

What an EMPTY STORE !

empty store sounds like **24**
4 × 6 = 24

4 X 7

The sailing boat was hired to a Summer Camp. Along came a little girl with a pony tail.

"Mmmm," said the little girl as soon as she got on board, "this sea air is making me feel hungry."

The sailing boat was not pleased to hear it.

"While I like most little girls," thought the boat, "I'm not sure that I trust this one. Maybe it's just the pony tail which makes her look naughty, but I have a feeling that if she finds the ship's biscuits, she will eat the lot."

So the sailing boat rocked about in the hope that the little girl would lose her appetite, but it did not work. She just grew hungrier and hungrier and soon decided to search the boat to see what she could find to eat.

She looked in all the lockers but she did not find the biscuits, only cups and saucers and dishes. She did not know the sailing boat was laughing.

"Oh dear," said the little girl, "I am so hungry I could eat an **empty plate**."

Eat away...

I am so hungry...

1 could eat an EMPTY PLATE!

empty plate sounds like **28**
4 × 7 = 28

4 x 8

The sailing boat had just been built and was waiting to make her first voyage. Along came a fat lady. She was carrying a huge bottle of champagne.

"Oh good," said the sailing boat, "she is going to name me by pouring champagne over my bows."

But the fat lady stood on the quayside and drank the whole bottle herself in one enormous swallow.

The sailing boat was most upset.

"How unfair," she thought. "I'm **thirsty too**."

mmm... quite nice!

I'm THIRSTY TOO!

thirsty too sounds like **32**
4 × 8 = 32

4 x 9

The sailing boat was taken to sea by a man with a big nose.

"I don't like the smell of this boat," said the man with the big nose. "I can't stand the smell of new paint."

The sailing boat felt very hurt. She was proud of her paintwork.

Then a storm blew up.

"Maybe he will get seasick," thought the boat.

But he did not; instead he got a terrible attack of the hiccups. Because of his big nose they came out extra loud. The boat laughed quietly.

"Take me back – hic," cried the man with the big nose, "I need – hic – a drink – hic."

But the sailing boat just smiled and pretended she did not understand.

"What shall I do?" cried the man with the big nose. "I can't drink sea water. Oh dear, I've got the **thirsty hics**."

He can drink sea water!

Oh ... hic ... dear ...

I've got the THIRSTY HICS!

thirsty hics sounds like **36**
4 × 9 = 36

The magic hen lays an egg next to everything it sees.

4 × 10 = 40

The terrible twins see everything double.

4 × 11 = 44

4 x 12

The sailing boat was taken out by the magician. The boat was sleepy and did not want to go for a sail. She was dozing and yawning and not taking any notice of what the magician was saying.

"If you don't improve," said the magician, "I'll turn you into something. You are in a very naughty state."

Because the sailing boat hadn't been concentrating she thought the magician had said "naughty skate".

"Oh, please don't turn me into a fish!" cried the boat.

The magician just laughed.

"That just shows you weren't listening. I didn't say naughty skate, I said **naughty state**."

I said NAUGHTY STATE.

*A skate is a kind of flat fish. All boats feel very superior to fish and they think that of all fish, the flat variety which swim around at the bottom of the sea, are to be despised the most.

naughty state sounds like **48**
4 × 12 = 48

The adventures of the man with the fat tummy

The man with the fat tummy met a ghost.
It made him disappear.

5 × 0 = 0

The man with the fat tummy looked in a mirror.
He admired himself and thought that his tummy looked splendid.

5 × 1 = 5

5 x 2

The man with the fat tummy was walking along by the river when he saw the swan.

"What a vain bird that is," he thought.

The swan noticed the man with the fat tummy at the same moment.

"Look at me," he said in a scornful voice. "Have you ever seen anything so beautiful? Aren't you sorry your tummy is so fat? Wouldn't you rather look like me?"

The man with the fat tummy was annoyed. He did not think it was his fault that he was fat. Then he smiled.

"Well," he said, "you seem a funny sort of shape to me."

"I'm not," said the swan indignantly.

"Your beak is too big," said the man with the fat tummy, trying not to laugh at the outraged expression on the swan's face. "Your neck is too long."

"It is not, it is not," cried the swan. "All swans have long necks."

"Oh, a swan," said the man with the fat tummy, pretending he had not known, "then that explains it. I thought you were a funny looking **hen**."

What a strange looking bird!

All swans have long necks.

I thought you were a HEN!

hen sounds like **10**

5 × 2 = 10

5 x 3

The man with the fat tummy was enjoying his favourite breakfast – four cans of baked beans on ten slices of toast – when along came the thin lady.

"Hello, Old Bean," she said, "you look very fit."

"Yes," laughed the man with the fat tummy, for he liked the thin lady. "I am a **fit bean**."

Yes, I am a FIT BEAN !

fit bean sounds like **15**
5 × 3 = 15

5 x 4

The man with the fat tummy thought he would like to sail in a sailing boat so he went to the harbour. There indeed was a sailing boat, but beside it was a notice saying, 'This boat is only suitable for three persons'.

"That sounds all right," said the man with the fat tummy. "I know I am heavy but I am only one person."

He climbed on board. The boat rocked violently and nearly went to the bottom.

The man with the fat tummy climbed out quickly.

"Three persons," he said, "what utter rubbish! What would have happened if someone else had been on board? Thank heavens the boat was **empty**."

Thank heavens it was EMPTY !

empty sounds like **20**
5 × 4 = 20

5 X 5

The man with the fat tummy went for a walk in the country with another man with a fat tummy. They were discussing food.

"I am so hungry," said the man with the fat tummy.

"So am I," said the other man with a fat tummy. "What I would really like is a nice piece of bread and lots and lots of honey."

Just then a bee buzzed by.

"Are you thinking what I am thinking?" asked the man with the fat tummy.

"Where there are bees, there is generally honey," said the other man with a fat tummy.

They followed the bee and came to a hive. They broke it open but there was no honey inside the hive.

"Oh no," groaned both men, "it's an **empty hive**."

I want to sting him on the tummy!

I can't run any faster!

All this for an EMPTY HIVE!

empty hive sounds like **25**
$$5 \times 5 = 25$$

5 x 6

The man with the fat tummy thought maybe he should do something about his weight, so he went to the doctor.

"You should go on a diet," said the doctor.

"What must I give up?" asked the man with the fat tummy.

"Everything," said the doctor. "You are to have no food and absolutely no drink."

"But," said the man with the fat tummy, "I would be **thirsty**."

Doctor! I will be THIRSTY!

thirsty sounds like **30**
5 × 6 = 30

5 X 7

The man with the fat tummy took his niece to a café. She was the little girl with the pony tail.

"You may have as much cola as you can drink," said the man with the fat tummy.

The little girl with the pony tail could only manage seven glasses. But the man with the fat tummy was enjoying himself. He kept on ordering more and more. In the end he finished 35 glasses of cola.

The little girl with the pony tail was very impressed.

"I didn't know it was possible to drink so much," she said. "I am going to call you **Thirsty Clive**."

I don't think I'll want another drink ever!

I'm going to call you THIRSTY CLIVE!

Thirsty Clive sounds like **35**
5 × 7 = 35

5 x 8

The man with the fat tummy was invited to a picnic. He and the fat lady were the first to arrive. There was lots to eat: cakes, buns, sandwiches, cookies, jellies, sausages, muffins and pies. They scoffed the whole lot before anybody else came.

"I enjoyed that," said the man with the fat tummy.

"So did I," said the fat lady, "but aren't we **naughty**!"

Aren't we NAUGHTY!

naughty sounds like **40**
5 × 8 = 40

5 X 9

The man with the fat tummy was most upset. He had been playing hide-and-seek with his wife but he couldn't find her. He asked the man with the big nose to help.

"I may be able to smell where she is," said the man with the big nose. "What does she smell like?"

"That's easy," said the man with the fat tummy, "she's always sucking peppermints."

The man with the big nose smelt the air.

"I can smell her," he said, "I can smell your **naughty wife**."

I can smell peppermint.

There's your NAUGHTY WIFE!

naughty wife sounds like **45**
5 × 9 = 45

The magic hen lays an egg next to every number it sees.

5 × 10 = 50

The terrible twins see everything double.

5 × 11 = 55

5 x 12

The man with the fat tummy was eating, as usual – this time pancakes with maple syrup. Along came the magician.

"Give me those pancakes," demanded the magician.

"No," said the man with the fat tummy, "I am going to eat them all myself."

"We'll see about that," said the magician and he took them by magic.

"But to show you I have a kind heart," he added, "I'll leave you the maple syrup."

He muttered a spell and the maple syrup poured itself all over the man with the fat tummy.

"Oh no," cried the man with the fat tummy, "I'm **sticky**."

I'll leave you the maple syrup!

Oh no, I'm STICKY!

sticky sounds like **60**
5 × 12 = 60

The adventures
of the doctor

The doctor met a ghost.
It made him disappear.

6 × 0 = 0

The doctor looked at himself in the mirror to see
if he had spots on his tongue. He saw himself and no spots.

6 × 1 = 6

6 x 2

The doctor was in the middle of a busy day in his surgery when in came the swan.

"Not another one who thinks I'm Dr Doolittle," thought the doctor. He glared at the swan.

"I'm not an animal doctor," he said.

"And I'm not an animal," said the swan proudly.

"I'm not a bird doctor either," said the doctor, "so you can just fly away."

"I haven't any energy," moaned the swan. "I need a tonic; I can't fly."

The doctor was not impressed.

"Time for the usual medicine," he thought.

He smiled: "I have just the tonic for you," he said.

He took out his gun from behind the door. The swan gave a loud squawk and flew straight out of the surgery window. The doctor laughed as he put the gun back.

"Best tonic I know," he said. "It always makes them **well**."

It always makes them WELL !

well sounds like **12**
6 × 2 = 12

6 x 3

The doctor was in his surgery when along came a thin lady.

"Doctor," she said, "I feel so faint."

The doctor looked at her. She really was much too thin.

"I'm not surprised," he said. "I don't believe you eat enough." And he asked her what she had eaten recently.

The doctor thought to himself: "This thin lady is proud of eating so little."

He reached for his prescription pad, and wrote down in his squiggly writing: one large meal four times a day.

He looked at the thin lady.

"Aren't you hungry?" he asked her.

"Yes," said the thin lady, giving him a pathetic look, "my stomach is **aching**."

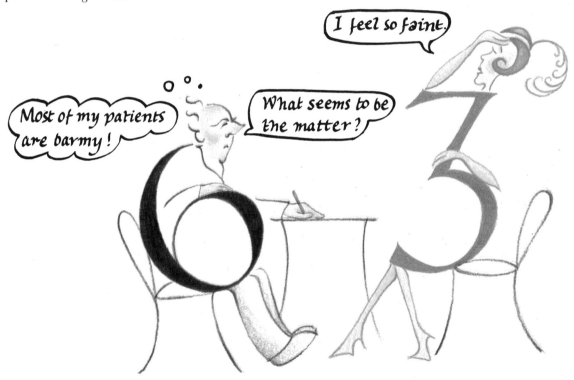

I feel so faint.

Most of my patients are barmy!

What seems to be the matter?

And my stomach is ACHING.

> **aching** sounds like **18**
> **6 × 3 = 18**

6 x 4

The doctor was feeling tired after seeing so many patients and thought he deserved a holiday. He took a sailing boat out to sea. He did not know that the sailing boat hated medical men. The sailing boat seemed to rock about a dreadful amount. Soon the poor doctor was feeling queasy.

"I must find the First Aid Box and have a sea sickness tablet," said the doctor.

He searched and at last found the First Aid Box. Inside there was only one aspirin, and also a used piece of sticking plaster.

"How disgusting!" said the doctor. "There is supposed to be a proper First Aid Box in the ship's stores. But this is an **empty store**."

I don't like doctors but this is embarrassing.

What an EMPTY STORE !

empty store sounds like **24**
6 × 4 = 24

6 x 5

The doctor was in his surgery when along came a man with a fat tummy.

"That man is really far too fat," thought the doctor.

"You should go on a diet," he told him.

The man with the fat tummy looked dreadfully sad.

"Oh doctor," he said, "what must I give up?"

"Everything," said the doctor crisply, for he had no patience with the overweight. "You must have no food and absolutely no drink."

"Doctor," cried the man with the fat tummy, "I will be **thirsty**."

Doctor! I will be THIRSTY!

thirsty sounds like **30**
6 × 5 = 30

6 x 6

The doctor went out to a smart restaurant with another doctor. They ordered a meal and the waiter put some bread rolls on the table. The first doctor was very hungry and straight away popped a whole bread roll into his mouth and swallowed it. Immediately he started to hiccup. Everybody in the restaurant turned to look at him.

"As a doctor, you should have known better," said the second doctor, "but we will soon put you right."

"Waiter," he called, "bring the doctor a glass of water.'

The waiter hurried off and brought back a glass of cool water complete with a little ice and lemon, for it was a very smart restaurant.

The doctor drank it and stopped hiccuping.

"I am really most surprised," said the second doctor. "As a doctor you should know that you should never eat bread so quickly and particularly without a drink. You had a classic case of what we doctors call the **thirsty hics**."

You had the THIRSTY HICS.

thirsty hics sounds like **36**
6 × 6 = 36

6 x 7

The doctor was in his surgery when in came a little girl with a pony tail. She looked familiar.

"Haven't I seen you somewhere before?" he said.

"Yes doctor," said the little girl with the pony tail, "I came to see you last week."

"Did you? Oh yes, perhaps you did," for like many doctors he was absent-minded. "What did you say your name was?"

"Susan" said the little girl with the pony tail.

"Why did you come to see me last week?" the doctor asked.

"Because I had a sore throat," said the little girl with the pony tail.

"Why have you come to see me this week?"

"I've still got a sore throat," said the little girl with the pony tail.

The doctor looked at his notes.

"Last week I gave you some medicine. Did you take it?"

"No," said the little girl with the pony tail, "it was absolutely disgusting."

"Tut tut," said the doctor. "No wonder you still have a sore throat, if you did not take your medicine. You are a very **naughty Sue**!"

You're a very NAUGHTY SUE!

naughty Sue sounds like **42**
6 × 7 = 42

6 x 8

The doctor was in his surgery when in came the fat lady. She looked as fat as ever.

"I don't believe you have been keeping to your diet," he said.

"Oh doctor, doctor," she cried, "I can't help it. It's my nerves, I get in such a state, such a terrible state if I don't have my cake."

"Nerves – rubbish," said the doctor. "State – rubbish. All you need is a little willpower. You have just got to remember that it is naughty cake and if you eat it, you are in a **naughty state**."

You are in a NAUGHTY STATE.

naughty state sounds like **48**
6 × 8 = **48**

6 X 9

The doctor was sitting in his surgery when in came the man with the big nose. His nose always looked big but today it was bright red as well.

"What have you done to your big nose," asked the doctor.

"I've hurt it, I've hurt it badly," cried the man with the big nose. He was most upset.

"How did you do it?" asked the doctor.

"I was just walking along," wailed the man with the big nose, "when I slipped on a **filthy floor**".

I slipped on a FILTHY FLOOR!

filthy floor sounds like **54**
6 × 9 = 54

The magic hen lays an egg next to every number it sees.

6 × 10 = 60

The terrible twins see everything double.

6 × 11 = 66

6 x 12

The doctor was in his surgery when in came the magician. He was looking green under his tall pointed hat.

"Doctor," said the magician, "I am feeling sick."

"I know what's the matter with you," said the doctor. "You have been eating that disgusting stew again. What do you put in it?"

"Nothing much," said the magician sheepishly (for he was a bit frightened of the doctor), "wing of bat, skin of toad . . . just that sort of thing."

"Now look," said the doctor, for he took no nonsense from his patients, particularly not the magician, "if you have to make it for your spells, then make it. But you must not, I repeat, must not eat it."

"And if you do," he added, "it is very likely to kill you one of these days and then you will just have to see how you like **heavenly stew**".

I wish I hadn't eaten that toad !

How would you like HEAVENLY STEW ?

heavenly stew sounds like **72**
6 × 12 = 72

The adventures of the little girl with the pony tail

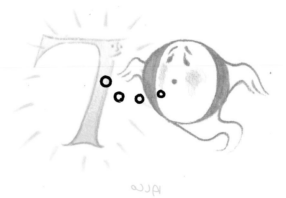

The little girl with the pony tail met a ghost;
it made her disappear.

7 × 0 = 0

The little girl wanted to see if the bow on her pony tail was straight.
She looked in the mirror and saw herself.

7 × 1 = 7

7 x 2

The little girl with the pony tail was playing by the river with her bow and arrows. She just couldn't shoot them straight. Suddenly she noticed the swan lying fast asleeep.

"It wouldn't miss a couple of tail feathers," she thought. "I'm sure they would help my arrows fly straight."

She crept up behind the swan and tugged out two large feathers. The swan woke immediately and to the little girl's horror started to give chase. He pecked her hard on the bottom. It really hurt.

"Don't! Stop it!" cried the little girl with the pony tail.

The swan pecked her again. The little girl was desperate to get away, so she said the first thing that came into her head.

"It wasn't me," she cried, "I didn't do anything."

"Who did then?" asked the swan.

The little girl smiled.

"It was Jean," she said, trying to hide the tail feathers that were still in her hand.

The swan paused and for a moment she thought he was going to go away. Then with a noise which sounded just like a laugh, he pecked her again.

"That one," he honked, "was **for Jean**."

If he pecks me again I'll cry!

That one was FOR JEAN !

for Jean sounds like **14**
7 × 2 = 14

7 x 3

The little girl with the pony tail went out to tea with the thin lady. They went to a lovely café and the little girl with the pony tail could see that lots of the other children there were eating ice cream and cakes and all sorts of delicious things. All the thin lady gave her was a glass of lemonade. It was very disappointing.

On the way home in the taxi the thin lady asked: "Did you have a nice time?"

"No," said the little girl with the pony tail, forgetting to be polite. "I've got an **empty tum**."

There's nothing to eat...

Oh, my EMPTY TUM !

empty tum sounds like **21**
7 × 3 = 21

7 X 4

The little girl with the pony tail went to Summer Camp and thought she would like to sail. She climbed on board a sailing boat and immediately felt hungry. She did not know that the sailing boat distrusted little girls in general and especially those with pony tails.

"I wonder if there is anything to eat on this boat," said the little girl, and started to look through all the lockers.

The boat rocked about but as the little girl did not know that it was doing it on purpose, she hardly noticed it. She just felt hungrier and hungrier.

"You'd have thought that there might be some ship's biscuits somewhere," said the little girl with the pony tail, "but all I can find are cups and saucers and dishes."

"Oh dear," she said, "I am so hungry I could eat an **empty plate**."

Eat away…

I am so hungry…

1 could eat an EMPTY PLATE!

empty plate sounds like **28**
7 × 4 = 28

7 x 5

The little girl with the pony tail was taken out by the man with the fat tummy – her Uncle Clive. He took her to a café and said she could have as much cola as she could drink.

"He's a pretty good uncle," she thought.

Although the little girl started drinking greedily she only managed seven bottles. But the man with the fat tummy kept on drinking and drinking and drinking.

"Wow," thought the little girl with the pony tail, "I didn't know anybody could drink that much."

"I know what I am going to call you," she laughed, "**Thirsty Clive**."

I don't think I'll want another drink ever!

I'm going to call you THIRSTY CLIVE!

Thirsty Clive sounds like **35**
7 × 5 = 35

7 x 6

The little girl with the pony tail was not feeling well so she went to the doctor.

The doctor looked at her and said: "Haven't I seen you somewhere before?"

The little girl went red.

"Yes, I came here last week."

"Yes," said the doctor, "perhaps you did. What is your name?"

"Susan," said the little girl with the pony tail.

"Why were you here last week?" asked the doctor.

"I had a sore throat," said the little girl.

"And why are you here this week?" the doctor asked.

"I've still got a sore throat," said the little girl. ("This is a very stupid doctor," she thought.)

The doctor looked at his notes.

"I gave you some medicine," he said, "did you take it?"

The little girl sighed; she had been afraid that he would ask her that.

"No," she said bravely, "it was disgusting."

The doctor looked very angry.

"Tut tut," he said. "No wonder you still have a sore throat, if you did not take your medicine. You are a very **naughty Sue**."

You're a very NAUGHTY SUE!

naughty Sue sounds like **42**
7 × 6 = 42

7 X 7

The little girl with the pony tail went to visit another little girl with a pony tail. They got up to all kinds of dreadful mischief and were sent to bed.

The other little girl's mother spoke severely to them.

"Now you are both to go to sleep; I want no fuss and absolutely no whining."

The little girls took no notice. They moaned, they groaned, they whined and they made a fuss.

The little girl's mother was losing patience. She shouted up the stairs.

"I told you two to be quiet and I meant it. I said no whining and what did I hear? I heard a **naughty whine**."

I heard a NAUGHTY WHINE.

naughty whine sounds like **49**
7 × 7 = 49

7 x 8

The little girl with the pony tail had the fat lady come to stay in her house. She found it very boring, for the fat lady did nothing but eat and sleep. The little girl with the pony tail decided that she would play a trick on her. She waited until the fat lady was asleep and then taking off her shoes, she crept up behind the fat lady and was about to shout "Boo" in a loud voice, when the fat lady woke up.

The fat lady looked at the little girl with the pony tail. She looked at the shoes that were dangling from her hand and she looked at her feet.

"Oh dear," thought the little girl with the pony tail, "she is going to be cross."

"Little girl," said the fat lady, "you have very **filthy socks**."

What FILTHY SOCKS!

filthy socks sounds like **56**
7 × 8 = 56

7 x 9

The little girl with the pony tail was walking down the road eating candy floss when she saw the man with the big nose. Never before had she seen a man with such a very large nose. She was fascinated. She turned to stare and quite forgot to look where she was going. She tripped, dropped her candy floss and somehow landed on top of it.

The man with the big nose helped her up.

"Are you all right?" he asked her.

"I suppose so," said the little girl with the pony tail, "but I've got a **sticky knee**."

Are you all right?

If he laughs, I'll shove this candy floss up his nose!

I've got a STICKY KNEE!

sticky knee sounds like **63**
7 × 9 = 63

The magic hen lays an egg next to every number it sees.

7 × 10 = 70

The terrible twins see everything double.

7 × 11 = 77

7 x 12

The little girl with the pony tail got 0 out of 100 in a maths test. She went to see the magician.

"Magician, you have got to help me," she said. "I just can't learn my tables."

Fortunately for her, the magician was in a good mood or else he might have turned her *into* a table.

"Don't worry," he said, "I will help you learn them through magic and then they won't be a **weighty chore**."

7 x 12 = 84

Now it's not a WEIGHTY CHORE.

weighty chore sounds like **84**
7 × 12 = 84

The adventures of the fat lady

The fat lady met a ghost
and it made her disappear.

8 × 0 = 0

One day the fat lady couldn't help looking
in the mirror; she saw herself.

8 × 1 = 8

8 x 2

The fat lady was sitting by the river with her toes in the water, dreaming of doughnuts and cream cakes. Suddenly she felt a terrible pain in her big toe. She looked down and there it was in the beak of the swan.

"Aggghhhh" she shrieked.

"I've never known fishes shriek before. What can it mean?" said the swan.

The fat lady thought the swan had an impertinent look about him.

"What does it mean?" she yelled, for her toe was still throbbing. "It means you pecked my toe."

She picked up a large stick and tried to hit the swan with it.

"Now I'm going to teach you something else. I'm going to teach you what **sticks mean**."

I've gone right off fish!

My poor toes!

I'll teach you what STICKS MEAN

sticks mean sounds like **16**
$8 \times 2 = 16$

8 x 3

The fat lady moved into a new house and was very pleased with the store cupboard which she soon filled with cakes. She invited the thin lady to come and see her new home. Then she remembered she had to pop out to post a letter.

Meanwhile the thin lady arrived. She was concerned about the birds in the garden.

"Poor things," she said, "they do look hungry. I wonder if I can find them anything to eat."

She found the fat lady's cupboard, with its store of cakes. Now the thin lady didn't like cakes, so she didn't try any. Her thoughts were for the birds.

"I think these cakes are rather stale," she said to herself, and she fed the lot to the sparrows.

The fat lady returned. All the way back she had been thinking of the banana gateau. You can imagine how upset she was to find it gone.

"Oh dear, oh dear," she cried, "look at my **empty store**!"

I'm sure this cake is stale...

Look at my EMPTY STORE!

empty store sounds like **24**
8 × 3 = 24

8 x 4

The fat lady was invited to launch a sailing boat. She went down to the quay where the boat was waiting. She was given an enormous bottle of champagne to throw over its bows. The fat lady looked at the boat.

"What a waste," she thought.

So she tipped up the bottle and drank it.

She did not stop to think about the sailing boat's feelings, but if she had listened she would have heard it say: "I'm **thirsty too**."

mmm... quite nice!

I'm THIRSTY TOO!

thirsty too sounds like **32**
8 × 4 = 32

8 x 5

The fat lady was invited to a picnic in the country. She arrived early and there waiting by the picnic hamper was the man with the fat tummy.

"I don't suppose," said the fat lady, "that it would matter very much if we tried a sandwich."

So they each had a sandwich and then a little cake and before they knew it they had eaten the whole lot.

"I enjoyed that," said the man with the fat tummy.

"So did I," said the fat lady, "but aren't we **naughty**!"

It's all gone!

Aren't we NAUGHTY!

naughty sounds like **40**
8 × 5 = 40

8 x 6

The fat lady went to see the doctor. She hadn't really wanted to go but her daughter made her. She went into the doctor's surgery and there he was, looking pleased with himself as usual.

"I don't believe you have been keeping to your diet," he said.

"Oh doctor," she cried, "I can't help it, it's my nerves. I get in a state, such a terrible state, if I don't have my cake."

The doctor did not look at all sympathetic.

"Nerves – rubbish, state – rubbish," he said. "All you need is a little willpower."

The fat lady had been afraid he would say that.

The doctor had not finished.

"All you need do is remember," he continued, "that it is naughty cake and if you eat it, you are in a **naughty state**."

You are in a NAUGHTY STATE.

naughty state sounds like **48**
8 × 6 = 48

8 x 7

The fat lady was staying at a house where there was a little girl with a pony tail. The wretched child was always playing tricks on her. No sooner had the fat lady gone to sleep than the little girl with the pony tail would wake her up.

One day the fat lady was settling down for a nap, her eyes were shut and she was just drifting off into a pleasant dream, when she heard the unmistakeable sound of someone creeping up behind her.

She jumped up as quickly as she could (which was not very quickly at all). And there, looking incredibly guilty was the little girl with the pony tail, holding her shoes in her hand.

The fat lady was just about to tell her off, when she heard the little girl's mother approaching. Now the fat lady was frightened of the little girl's mother, so she simply said in a meaningful voice: "What **filthy socks**!"

WHAT FILTHY SOCKS!

filthy socks sounds like **56**
8 × 7 = 56

8 X 8

The fat lady met her very special friend – another fat lady. They went into a sweet shop together and bought a large packet of toffee.

Then they went to sit in the park to eat it.

"This toffee is really good," said the first fat lady.

"Wuu wuu wer wer," said the second fat lady.

"I beg your pardon?" said the first fat lady.

"Wuu wuu wer wer," said the second fat lady again.

The first fat lady was worried about her friend. What could be the matter?

"Wu we" said the second fat lady pathetically.

Then the first fat lady understood the problem.

"I know what is the matter with you," she said. "Your jaw is stuck together. You have got a **sticky jaw**."

You've got a STICKY JAW.

sticky jaw sounds like **64**
8 × 8 = 64

8 X 9

The fat lady was cooking a stew, when who should arrive but the man with the big nose.

"I can smell something wonderful," he said.

"I'm sure you can't," said the fat lady. She did not want to share her supper.

But the man with the big nose pushed straight past her and went to the stove.

He lifted the lid of one of the saucepans and found the stew.

"Ah, what's this?" he asked.

"Nothing," said the fat lady, "nothing at all."

"If it's nothing," said the man with the big nose, "you won't mind me eating it."

The poor fat lady watched sadly as the man with the big nose ate her supper.

"I'm surprised you called that nothing," he said. "I would call it stew, and if I may compliment you, a really **heavenly stew**."

It was my supper!

It's a HEAVENLY STEW !

heavenly stew sounds like **72**
8 × 9 = 72

The magic hen lays an egg next to every number it sees.

8 × 10 = 80

The terrible twins see everything double.

8 × 11 = 88

8 x 12

The fat lady was just going to bed when there was a knock at the door. She answered it and there stood the magician.

"I want a room for the night," demanded the magician.

"I'm sorry," said the fat lady, "but I am not a boarding house or an hotel. I do not take lodgers of any kind."

The magician looked furious.

"Nobody says no to the magician," he roared.

The fat lady felt quite frightened; she suddenly realised that she might have made a mistake.

"Oh dear," she thought, "if he turns me into something, I do hope it's something nice."

She stood there waiting, with her eyes shut.

But the magician couldn't think of anything, so he broke the shoulder straps of her nightdress by magic. The fat lady's nightdress fell to her knees, and she went bright red.

She looked so funny that the magician burst out laughing.

"Excuse me," he said, pretending to be polite, "I don't know whether you've noticed but your **nightie's slipped**."

Your NIGHTIE'S SLIPPED!

nightie's slipped sounds like **96**
8 × 12 = 96

The adventures of the man with the big nose

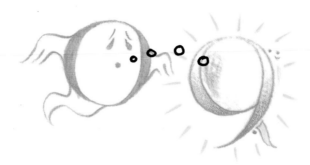

The man with the big nose met a ghost.
It made him disappear.

9 × 0 = 0

The man with the big nose wondered if his nose was
redder than usual. He looked in the mirror and saw himself.

9 × 1 = 9

9 x 2

The man with the big nose had been working hard and so he decided to take a walk by the river. After a bit he felt sleepy, lay down in a clump of grass and fell fast asleep. He woke up with a terrible pain in his nose. Then he saw the swan looking very embarrassed.

"I'm terribly sorry," it muttered "I thought you were a snoring poppy. I do hope your nose doesn't hurt too much."

The man with the big nose felt a little sorry for the swan as it did look ashamed. But his nose *was* sore.

"Well, it does hurt," he said gruffly. "Thanks to you, it's **aching**."

It's ACHING.

aching sounds like **18**
9 × 2 = 18

9 x 3

The man with the big nose was going for a walk in the country when, under a tree, fast asleep, he saw a thin lady. She looked so pretty, the man with the big nose decided that he would try to kiss her. He crept up beside her and bent over, but the feather in her hat tickled his big nose and he let out a most enormous sneeze.

The thin lady woke up immediately.

"Oh my," she said, "I had the most terrible dream."

"What did you dream?" asked the man with the big nose.

"I dreamt I went to heaven and I was the only person there," said the thin lady.

"You poor thing," said the man with the big nose, "you dreamt you were in an **empty heaven**."

You were in an EMPTY HEAVEN.

empty heaven sounds like **27**
9 × 3 = 27

9 x 4

The man with the big nose took a sailing boat out to sea. As soon as they left the shore the man with the big nose realised he did not trust the sailing boat.

"I do not like the smell of this boat. I can't stand the smell of new paint and what is more I believe it has a tricky nature," he said.

He found the boat very difficult to control. The wind grew stronger and the waves became higher and the poor man with the big nose got a terrible attack of the hiccups.

He tried to get the boat back to shore, but it seemed to take no notice.

"Oh what can I do?" cried the poor man with the big nose. "I need a drink – hic, a drink – hic. I can't drink sea water – hic. I do want to get rid of these **thirsty hics**."

I've got the THIRSTY HICS!

thirsty hics sounds like **36**
9 × 4 = 36

9 x 5

The man with the big nose came across the man with the fat tummy looking worried.

"Oh, I wonder if you can help me," said the man with the fat tummy. "I was playing hide-and-seek with my wife and now I can't find her."

"Don't worry" said the man with the big nose. "I may be able to smell her. What does she smell like?"

"That's easy," said the man with the fat tummy. "She is like me, a little on the tubby side and that is partly because she is always sucking peppermints."

Now, it so happened that the man with the big nose had been puzzled by the smell of peppermint ever since he had walked down this particular path. He sniffed the air, turned round three times and then pointed to a hollow tree.

"There she is," he cried. "I can smell your **naughty wife**."

I can smell peppermint.

There's your NAUGHTY WIFE!

naughty wife sounds like **45**
9 × 5 = 45

9 x 6

The man with the big nose hurt his poor nose very badly and went to see the doctor. In the waiting room he tried to cover his nose with newspaper because he was embarrassed.

When it was finally his turn, the doctor took one look at him and said: "What have you done to your nose?"

"I've hurt it," said the man with the big nose, thinking that this really should be obvious to someone who was supposed to have been medically trained.

"How did you do it?" asked the doctor.

The man with the big nose sighed, for he knew that people found his accident extremely funny.

"It was like this," he said. "I slipped on a **filthy floor**."

I slipped on a FILTHY FLOOR!

filthy floor sounds like **54**
9 × 6 = 54

9 x 7

The man with the big nose was walking down the street when he noticed a little girl with a pony tail licking candy floss. She seemed to be staring at him in an exceptionally rude way. The man with the big nose felt sad. People often stared at him because of his big nose and he did not like it one bit.

Just as he was wishing that she might grow a big nose and find out what it felt like, the little girl with the pony tail tripped over and landed on top of her candy floss.

"Are you all right?" he asked her, trying not to laugh (although he was actually very pleased because it was usually he himself who fell over).

"I suppose so," said the little girl with the pony tail, "but I've got a **sticky knee**."

sticky knee sounds like **63**
9 × 7 = 63

9 x 8

The man with the big nose went to see the fat lady. He was very angry with her because he knew that she had been raiding his kitchen garden.

When he arrived he could smell a delicious smell. His big nose told him that it was a stew containing all his own vegetables: carrots, onions, celery, peas and beans.

"Ah," said the man with the big nose, "I can smell something. What are you cooking?"

"Nothing, nothing at all," said the fat lady, as he knew she would.

"I will just come in for a coffee," said the man with a big nose. He marched into the kitchen and soon smelt out the stew.

All the time he kept a straight face and all the time the poor fat lady just protested that it was nothing, nothing at all.

"I will teach her a lesson," thought the man with the big nose and he ate the whole of the stew.

"You are too modest," he said. "I don't call that nothing. It was a stew and if I may compliment you on your cooking, a **heavenly stew**."

It was my supper!

It's a HEAVENLY STEW !

heavenly stew sounds like **72**
9 × 8 = 72

9 X 9

The man with the big nose met another man with a big nose – his twin brother.

"How are you?" asked the other man with the big nose.

"Very well," said the first man with the big nose.

"You don't look very well," said the second man with the big nose. "For one thing, your nose is far too big. I am surprised you don't keep falling over."

The man with the big nose was upset, particularly as he did fall over rather a lot.

"Talk about *my* big nose!" he said. "Have you looked at your own nose in the mirror recently? You've got a **weighty one**."

Your nose is too big!

You've got a WEIGHTY ONE !

weighty one sounds like **81**
$$9 \times 9 = 81$$

The magic hen lays an egg next to every number it sees.

$$9 \times 10 = 90$$

The terrible twins see everything double.

$$9 \times 11 = 99$$

9 x 12

The man with the big nose was in a terrible hurry. He was rushing down the street, when he bumped into the magician. His big nose sent the magician flying.

"Where do you think you are going?" demanded the magician. "Look, you have ruined my best cloak."

"I'm sorry," said the man with the big nose, "but I was in a hurry."

"Hurry! You hurry far too much if you ask me," said the magician. "But I'm going to stop you hurrying; I am going to turn you into an old man of **one hundred, and** you will be **late**."

I don't think I like him very much.

ONE HUNDRED AND *you'll be* LATE !

one hundred and late sounds like **108**
9 × 12 = 108

The adventures
of the magic hen

Whenever the hen met another number, she just could not resist laying an egg.

She saw the ghost and rushed up to him, hoping to lay an egg. But he made her disappear.

$$10 \times 0 = 0$$

She saw the mirror and, reflected in the glass, she saw herself and her egg.

$$10 \times 1 = 10$$

The magic hen met the swan. She liked the swan and laid a golden egg next to him.

$$10 \times 2 = 20$$

The magic hen saw the thin lady, smiled and laid an egg next to her.

$$10 \times 3 = 30$$

In fact the magic hen laid an egg next to every number she saw.

$$10 \times 4 = 40$$
$$10 \times 5 = 50$$
$$10 \times 6 = 60$$
$$10 \times 7 = 70$$
$$10 \times 8 = 80$$
$$10 \times 9 = 90$$

When she met another hen with an egg, the magic hen gave a cluck and laid an egg next to it.

$$10 \times 10 = 100$$

The magic hen met the terrible twins, smiled and laid an egg next to them.

$$10 \times 11 = 110$$

Even with very big numbers, the magic hen just carried on laying eggs.

$$10 \times 45 = 450$$
$$10 \times 136 = 1,360$$
$$10 \times 5,275 = 52,750$$

The adventures
of the terrible twins

The terrible twins were always up to mischief!

One day they saw the ghost.

   "Come on, let's tease him," said one twin.

   But before they could get up to any mischief, the ghost made the twins disappear.

$$11 \times 0 = 0$$

The twins came across the mirror and looked into it. They saw two terrible twins grinning back at them.

$$11 \times 1 = 11$$

"We're double trouble!" they laughed.

In fact they went on to see everything double.

$$11 \times 2 = 22$$
$$11 \times 3 = 33$$
$$11 \times 4 = 44$$
$$11 \times 5 = 55$$
$$11 \times 6 = 66$$
$$11 \times 7 = 77$$
$$11 \times 8 = 88$$
$$11 \times 9 = 99$$

The terrible twins saw everything double until they came to the magic hen.

   The magic hen was not impressed by double-seeing twins. She just laid an egg next to them.

$$11 \times 10 = 110$$

When the terrible twins met another pair of terrible twins, they started quarrelling and very soon got into a terrible fight.

After a while two of the twins stopped fighting, but the other two carried on. They tied themselves in a terrible knot.

$$11 \times 11 = 121$$

Exhausted after all this fighting, the twins saw the magician walking towards them. The magician looked at them.

"I'm going to cast a spell on you," said the magician. "It will give you powers over numbers you meet."

"When you meet a number made of two parts such as 14 or 36 or 72, you tie one part of the number to one tree, and one part to another tree. (This is so that they can't get away.) Then you look at the two parts, add them together, and put the answer in the middle."

$$11 \times 14 = 154$$
$$11 \times 72 = 792$$

"Oh," said the twins, "that will be useful."

One of the terrible twins thought a bit.

"But what happens when we meet a number like 77 or 68 or 55?" he said. "If we add the two parts of the number together and it comes to 10, or more than 10, what do we do then?"

"Ah," sighed the magician, "nothing in life is quite as simple as it might be. Try and work out what happens."

But the terrible twins couldn't be bothered and ran off.

$$11 \times 63 = 693$$

The adventures of the magician

The magician met the ghost
and it made him disappear.

$$12 \times 0 = 0$$

The magician looked in the mirror to see if it was magic.
It did not tell him anything; all he saw was himself.

$$12 \times 1 = 12$$

12 x 2

The magician had a particularly interesting spell he wanted to try out. The only problem was that it needed some rather tricky ingredients which took a long time to collect. Into his cauldron went some wing of bat, some old socks, some reindeer's teeth, a piece of cheese, five eyelashes and a spoonful of castor oil. Then he went off to the marsh, to collect the final items. He had just put in the newt spit, the frogspawn and the duckweed, when he saw the swan listening to him.

"Wretched creature," he thought, "I don't want him knowing my secrets."

Then he decided to play a trick on the swan.

"All I need for my store of ingredients, is a swan's tongue," he said and grabbed at the swan.

The swan struggled wildly.

"Stupid bird," thought the magician, "can't take a joke."

He was just about to let the bird go and have a good laugh, when the swan struggled free, upsetting the cauldron. This time the magician really was furious.

"You stupid bird," he roared, "I've a good mind to turn you into something. Look what you've done, look at my **empty store**!"

Look at my EMPTY STORE !

empty store sounds like **24**
12 × 2 = 24

12 x 3

The magician went out for a walk, and he saw the thin lady. She was having a drink of low calorie lemonade. Everything about the thin lady annoyed the magician: the way she sipped the lemonade with dainty little sips and the way she put her little finger out as she held the glass. And he didn't like her hat. Looking at the thin lady, the magician felt thirsty himself.

"Give me that lemonade," he demanded as was his custom when he felt in a bad mood.

The thin lady refused so the magician took it by magic.

"Oh," said the thin lady "but I am thirsty."

The magician did not like her voice: it was rather high pitched and squeaky.

"I don't care," he laughed. "You should have given it to me straight away, and to punish you I am going to give you hiccups as well. Then you will have the **thirsty hics**."

Oh no, not the THIRSTY HICS!

thirsty hics sounds like **36**
12 × 3 = 36

12 x 4

The magician went for a sail in a sailing boat. It was a beautiful day but the boat seemed very slow and sluggish.

"I don't know what's wrong with this boat," thought the magician, "but she seems half asleep."

He was in a good mood that day so he didn't really mind. All the same he would have liked to go a little faster.

"If you don't improve," he said casually to the boat, "I will turn you into something. You are in a very naughty state."

The magician had not really thought the boat would take any notice, but to his amazement the boat filled out her sails and shot across the water.

"Oh, please don't turn me into a fish," she said in alarm.

The magician laughed.

"That just shows you weren't listening," he said. "I didn't say naughty skate, I said you were in a very **naughty state**."

1 said NAUGHTY STATE.

naughty state sounds like **48**
12 × 4 = 48

12 x 5

The magician was walking along when he saw the man with the fat tummy eating pancakes. It was a disgusting sight! First he covered them in maple syrup, then he crammed them into his mouth two at a time. The magician thought he would teach him some table manners.

"Give me those pancakes," he demanded.

"No," said the man with the fat tummy, "I'm going to eat them all myself."

"We'll see about that," said the magician, and he took the pancakes by magic.

"Now to make the picture complete," he laughed, "I will leave you the maple syrup."

The maple syrup poured itself over the man with the fat tummy.

"Oh dear," said the man with the fat tummy, "now I'm **sticky**."

I'll leave you the maple syrup!

Oh no, I'm STICKY!

sticky sounds like **60**
12 × 5 = 60

12 x 6

The magician was feeling rather sick, so he went to the doctor.

The doctor took one look at him and said: "I know what's the matter with you. You have been eating that disgusting stew again. What do you put in it?"

The magician turned from green to red. He liked to think his stews were a secret.

"Oh, wing of bat, skin of toad, that sort of thing," he said.

"Well," said the doctor briskly, "if you have to make it for your spells, then make it. But you must not, I will repeat, must not eat it."

The magician sighed. He hated being told off by the doctor.

The doctor had not finished.

"If you do," he continued, "it will kill you one of these days and then you will just have to see how you like **heavenly stew**."

I wish 1 hadn't eaten that toad !

How would you like HEAVENLY STEW ?

heavenly stew sounds like **72**
12 × 6 = 72

12 x 7

The magician was planning some new spells, when he saw the little girl with the pony tail. She seemed very sad.

"You must help me," she said. "I can't learn my tables and we've got another maths test tomorrow and I know I'm going to come bottom again."

The magician looked at her kindly; he remembered when he was a boy, his old mother the witch had made him learn his tables and had refused to give him any magic help.

"Don't worry," he said, "I will help you learn your tables through magic and then it won't be such a **weighty chore**."

7 × 12 = 84

Now it's not a WEIGHTY CHORE.

weighty chore sounds like **84**
12 × 7 = 84

12 x 8

The magician went out for a walk but he quite forgot the time and found that by nightfall he had wandered a long way from home. He knocked on the fat lady's door.

"I would like a room for the night," he told her.

The fat lady looked insulted.

"I am not a boarding house or an hotel. I take no lodgers of any kind," she said in a haughty voice.

The magician was furious.

"Nobody says no to the magician," he roared.

He wondered what he could turn her into, but really nothing seemed to him more ridiculous than the fat lady just the way she was. So he broke the shoulder straps of her nightdress by magic. The nightdress slipped down to the fat lady's knees and she turned bright red.

"Excuse me," said the magician roaring with laughter, "I don't know whether you've noticed, but your **nightie's slipped**".

I've never been so embarrassed.

I've never seen anything so funny!

Your NIGHTIE'S SLIPPED!

nightie's slipped sounds like **96**
12 × 8 = 96

12 x 9

The magician was walking along the road minding his own business when along came the man with the big nose, who was not looking where he was going. He bumped straight into the magician and knocked him over. The magician picked himself up.

"Where do you think you are going?" he demanded. "Look, you have ruined my best cloak."

"I'm sorry," said the man with the big nose, "but I was in a hurry."

The magician thought that was a pathetic excuse. "Hurry!" he said. "I think you hurry far too much. But I'm going to stop that – see just how much hurrying you can do now!"

He turned the man with the big nose into an old man of one hundred.

"Ah ha," laughed the magician, "now you will be **one hundred and late**."

I don't think I like him very much.

ONE HUNDRED AND *you'll be* LATE!

one hundred and late sounds like **108**
12 × 9 = 108

The magician was walking along the road when he met the magic hen.

"Bird magic," snorted the magician, "feeble stuff."

He was wrong; the magic hen was more powerful than he was and simply laid an egg next to him.

12 × 10 = 120

12 x 11

The magician was feeling tired, when who should come along but the terrible twins. He had already tried to teach them magic and did not feel like doing it again.

"I bet they've forgotten all I taught them," he sighed.

"What's the answer to 11 × 12?" he asked them.

But the twins were too busy being terrible. They could not remember what they had to do.

"I've lost patience with you two," said the magician. "I am going to turn you into old men of **one hundred and** just to help you remember next time I'm going to make you **thirsty too**."

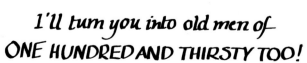

I'll turn you into old men of
ONE HUNDRED AND THIRSTY TOO!

one hundred and thirsty two sounds like **132**
12 × 11 = 132

12 x 12

The magician met another magician and soon they got talking about all the spells they had cast on people.

"The other day I made somebody one hundred," said the magician.

"I've done that," said the other magician. "I wonder what it's like to be one hundred. Let's find out."

"I don't know whether we should," said the first magician. "Once, when I was a boy, I turned myself into a beetle and my mother nearly put me into her cauldron. I promised her then that I would never turn myself into things, and I suppose I still feel that it is naughty."

"Don't be so pathetic," said the second magician, "you are grown up now."

The first magician finally agreed and they both turned themselves into old men of one hundred. It was very boring indeed.

"Naughty!" said the second magician, when they had safely turned back. "Did that really feel naughty?"

"Well," said the first magician, "it was a naughty bore – **one hundred and naughty bore**."

This is ONE HUNDRED AND NAUGHTY BORE.

one hundred and naughty bore sounds like **144**
12 × 12 = 144

The numbers

You can cut out these pictures and stick them onto card to make flash cards.
Use the cards when you are introducing the characters and also as prompts later on.

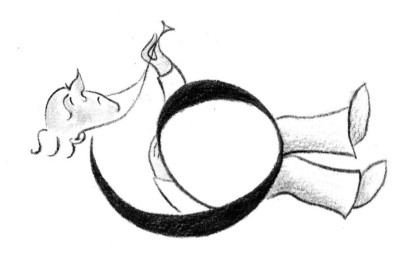

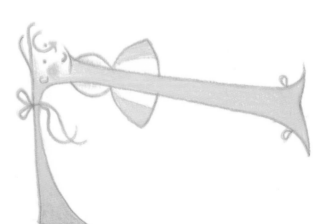

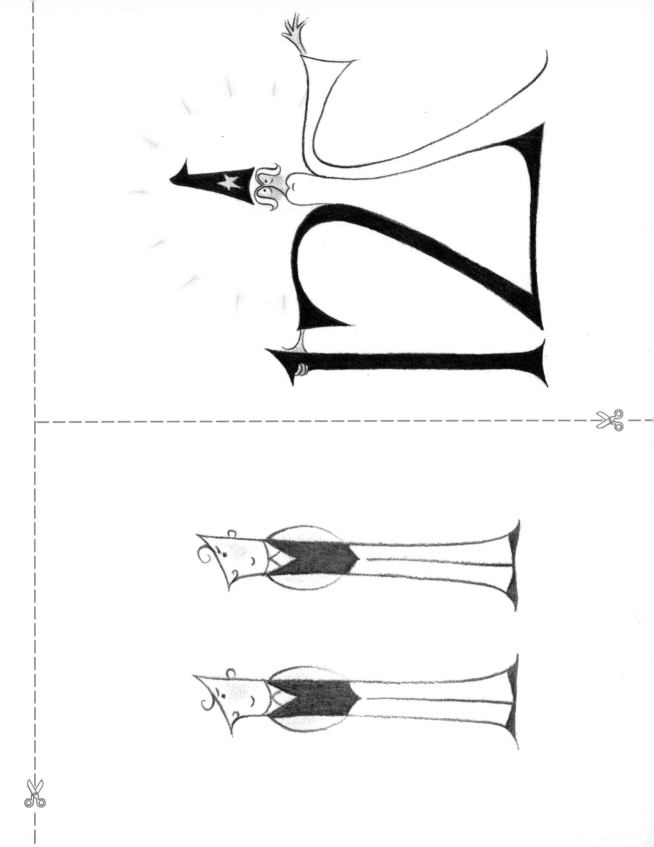

Notes
for parents

Table Time is a story book with a difference – it makes learning and revising tables fun! It is a modified version of the system I devised for my daughter, who had been trying, without much success, to learn her tables for a whole year. She had been set table-learning homework, given table tests at school and had been nagged by her teachers. It seemed to me, that as fast as she learnt one set of tables, she forgot another. Her failure was not only seriously affecting her maths performance but making her hate maths in general. Using the Table Time method she learnt all her tables over the space of one weekend, and retained that knowledge.

The system is based on thought association. All the numbers have characters that have different adventures. Each story ends with a punch line which children find as easy to remember as the punch line of playground jokes. The punch line in turn reminds them of the correct answer to each multiplication sum. Using traditional learning methods, children often have to run through the whole table to get to the answer they need. Using this method they are able to pick out the right answer when the tables are dotted about, just as easily as when they are in their proper order.

How to use this book

DO NOT START BEFORE YOUR CHILD IS READY

Table Time simply takes the hard work out of memorizing tables; it does not teach the principles of multiplication. So it is important not to try to teach your child until he is familiar with the whole concept of counting in twos and counting in tens, and is able to do simple multiplication sums with the use of table sheets. Children who are still having problems with addition and subtraction can easily become confused if you do try to move on to tables too soon. But you will almost certainly know when your child is ready: he will probably be moaning about his table test.

What to do

Cut out the flash cards and go through the numbers slowly. Make sure that the child recognizes what each character represents. Most children learn this rapidly and the flash cards reinforce that process.

Next, go through the adventure of just one number. Give the child plenty of time to look at the pictures and make sure he understands any new words. Occasionally the child may need the punch lines explained.

Stop, after having gone through three or four picture stories, and check that the child has memorized the punch lines. Do not at this stage ask the question in mathematical terms such as, "What is 3 × 8?", but rather by asking a question which reminds the child of the story. Hold up the flash cards and ask, "What did the fat lady (that's eight) say when the thin lady (that's three) threw her cake to the birds?" If the child can not give the answer, prompt with half the punch line, "Oh my empty . . .?" Often the child will add "Store". You then say, "Yes, that is twenty four." Do not leave the child trying to remember the story for more than a few seconds: you are aiming at instant recall. Instead show him the picture again.

Once he has reached the stage where he can think of the punch line when reminded of the story, you move on to asking the question in numbers. Expect the child to pause for a couple of seconds while he translates the numbers into the characters and remembers the story. Again be quick to prompt with the flash cards if he looks as if he is having problems. The whole point of this method is to build confidence. You will find that the child will progress very quickly from giving that slight pause before an answer to being able to give the correct answer immediately.

This method sounds more time-consuming than it is. It has the great advantage that once the child has memorized a punch line, it will stick in his mind, whereas it is all too easy for a child who learns his tables in the conventional way, to appear to remember a table and then forget it the next day.

How quickly your child will recall the situations will, of course, vary. A few children will be able to do so almost instantly, others will take a little longer, but most children will enjoy this method. It is important to keep it that way. Stop immediately if your child's attention starts to wander, and in any case after about twenty minutes. You are quite likely to find that he will come to you later in the day to learn some more.

Some children, particularly if they are confident readers, will just want to take the book away and learn the stories by themselves. As long as they are enjoying it, this can be encouraged. Do remember that most children take a year, at least, to learn all their tables. While there will be those who will learn all the stories and their punch lines in a couple of days, others may need a few weeks or even a month or two. Even if Table Time teaches your child in just half the time that it would otherwise have taken, it must be worth it.